StevieW★nder

text	**Sam Hasegawa**
illustrations	**Dick Brude**
design concept	**Mark Landkamer**

| published by | **Creative Education**
Mankato, Minnesota |

Published by Creative Educational Society, Inc.,
123 South Broad Street, Mankato, Minnesota 56001
Copyright © 1975 by Creative Educational Society, Inc. International
copyrights reserved in all countries.
No part of this book may be reproduced in any form without written permission
from the publisher. Printed in the United States.
Distributed by Childrens Press, 1224 West Van Buren Street, Chicago, Illinois 60607
ISBN 0-87191-395-X
Library of Congress Cataloging in Publication Data
Hasegawa, Sam.   Stevie Wonder.
SUMMARY: A biography of the blind black musician who from
early childhood showed signs of the talent that has
made him one of America's most popular performers.
1. Wonder, Stevie—Juvenile literature.
[1. Wonder, Stevie. 2. Musicians, American. 3. Negroes—Biography]
I. Brude, Dick, illus.   II. Title.
ML3930.W65H4   784'.092'4 [B] [92]   74-14746

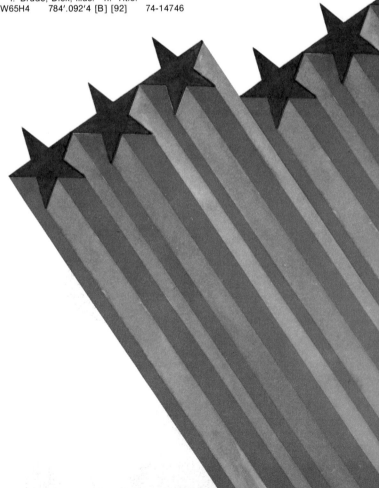

In Concert

In the summer of 1972 the Rolling Stones were on tour in America for the first time in over 2 years. The Stones swept across the country, playing to sellout crowds wherever they appeared. It was one of the most sensational tours in the history of rock music.

The only other act on the program was Stevie Wonder and his band, Wonderlove. At first, few people seemed aware that Stevie was part of the tour. All the attention was focused on the legendary Stones.

Yet after a few concerts, Stevie made his presence felt dramatically. Audiences discovered the tremendous impact of his music. People impatient to hear the Rolling Stones were suddenly surprised to find themselves totally caught up in the joy and magic of Stevie's performances.

On June 18th the tour arrived in Bloomington, Minnesota, a suburb of Minneapolis. The crowd filling the Metropolitan Sports Center was like many other audiences on the tour. Most of the people had come just to hear the Rolling Stones. But like the audiences in other cities, they were about to experience something they had not really counted on — the genius of Stevie Wonder.

Inside the Sports Center, the anticipation of thousands of people charged the air with electricity. The air-conditioning had broken down. As the excitement mounted, the temperature soared into the 90's.

The setting did not quite match the concert atmosphere. The arena was designed as a place to view basketball or hockey games. For the concert, the scoreboard and the basketball backboards had been raised toward the ceiling. But they were still visible.

In the excitement, however, few people noticed them.

Everyone's attention was directed toward the stage and its equipment.

The cylindrical shapes of the drums, golden cymbals and chrome mike stands flashed at both sides of a cluster of electronic keyboard instruments.

To the rear were the amplifiers — a somber wall of grey grill cloth topped with panels of switches and knobs that stretched the length of the stage.

Two massive black columns, towering 18 feet above the arena floor, flanked this array of equipment. They were the Stones' PA system, twin stacks of speaker enclosures housing a total of 150 speakers.

The presence of all this equipment transformed the arena into a fantasy land — a bizarre combination of sports arena and concert hall. It seemed like something out of a dream. But as the house lights began to dim, the details of the sports arena faded from view. The stage was flooded with the brilliant, rainbow-colored beams of spotlights. And suddenly, the place had become a concert hall.

The emcee, dwarfed by the equipment, was on stage announcing Wonderlove. It was a big band: 2 guitars, bass, drums, congas and 3 horns. They came out, without Stevie, to do an instrumental. The sound was big and brassy, sparked by explosive interplay between the drummer and the conga player.

Then the band quietly eased into another song. Stevie, dressed in a flowing African robe, came into view. On the arm of one of his 3 girl singers, he made his way across the stage, smiling and waving to the crowd. His head was rocking from side to side with the music.

Seated at his keyboard instruments, Stevie began to play. His solos inspired the band to a higher level of

excitement. The music seemed suddenly transformed; the sound became totally different.

For one thing, in addition to electric piano, Stevie was playing a synthesizer. Its piercing, siren-like notes floated eerily through the air. Stevie loved this electronic keyboard instrument. Through its electronic circuits, the synthesizer generates an amazing variety of musical sounds. It can be programmed to imitate the tones of any musical instrument. But it is often used to create pure electronic sounds which are totally unique.

Then there was Stevie's singing, more flexible and expressive than ever. The dark, husky sound of his vocals made warm spirals of melody. His singing intertwined beautifully with the electronic cries of the synthesizer and the bright, clear voices of the girl singers.

The show built steadily in intensity. As it neared its climax, Stevie jumped up and headed back toward the drums. Taking the drummer's place, Stevie began to play. All the musicians, except the conga player, dropped out. The intricate rhythms of drums and congas crackled like a smouldering fire. The crowd began to clap in time to the music. Stevie's sticks flew faster over the drums. The volume swelled. And suddenly the music flared up into explosions of percussive fireworks.

The deep thud of the bass drum, the blur of snare drum rolls, the high-pitched rhythms of the congas, the shimmering ring of cymbal crashes — all reverberated in the bright orange glare of the spotlights.

Then at Stevie's signal the rest of the band came in. An overpowering sound burst from the hundreds of speakers. The heavy vibrations of the bass merged with the percussion. The twisting notes of the electric guitar soared through the fragments of melody punched out by the brass.

Stevie was now out front singing, his whole body swaying from side to side. The music, a burning flood of emotion, rushed out, engulfing the crowd. And everyone floated on the same glowing level, held up by the energy of the sound.

Twelve Year Old Genius

Stevie's musical talent had its roots in the Detroit ghetto where he was raised. The third of 6 children, he was born Steveland Morris on May 13, 1950. His family was, in his own words, "upper-lower-class." His father was seldom around.

Blind from birth, Stevie grew up in a world of sounds: the rhythm and blues tunes he heard on the radio; the gospel music of the churches he attended; the performances of street corner musicians; the varied noises of the street itself.

Stevie was gifted with extremely sensitive hearing. If someone would drop a coin on the floor, Stevie could tell instantly what kind it was by the sound it made.

He showed an ear for music at an early age. When he was 2, he began to beat on pans and dishes in time to music. His first chance to play real drums came at a picnic. A band was performing in the park where Stevie and his family were eating, and he began to play along, banging out a beat with 2 spoons.

The band's drummer saw that Stevie had good rhythm. He asked Stevie if he would like to play the drums with the band. Stevie was so small that he had to sit on the drummer's lap to reach the drums. But he played so well that a crowd began to form around the bandstand.

When the tune was over, Stevie was surprised to hear applause and the sound of coins bouncing off the drums as his audience showered the stage with money.

After that, Stevie got a set of toy drums every Christmas. He played them so hard that they were usually demolished within a few weeks.

He received his first real instrument, a small harmonica, when he was 5. While he was teaching himself how to play it, he also began to take up piano. Later, this first harmonica was replaced by a larger chromatic model. And finally, at age 9, Stevie got his first real drum. It was a snare drum donated by a charity for blind children.

Stevie learned music by listening to the radio and imitating the music he liked. He copied the styles of rhythm and blues singers like Jackie Wilson and Ray Charles, his idol. As he got better at it, he began to develop a vocal style all his own.

Stevie had his own ideas about how the harmonica should be played. He did not imitate blues harpists (harmonica is also called harp). Instead, he listened to the solos of rhythm and blues saxophonist King Curtis and learned to play them on the harmonica.

Stevie began to liven up the neighborhood with concerts for his friends. One of his regular listeners was the younger brother of Ronnie White, a singer in the famous rhythm and blues group, the Miracles. Stevie was at the White's one day, when Ronnie happened to stop in. It was the first time he had heard Stevie playing harmonica and singing. Greatly impressed, Ronnie arranged an audition for Stevie at Tamla Motown, the Miracles' recording company.

There Stevie did some rhythm and blues standards and a few songs he had written himself. Motown president

Berry Gordy wasted no time in making a decision. Stevie, then 10 years old, came out with a 5-year recording contract and a new name: Little Stevie Wonder.

In 1963 Stevie cut his fourth 45, "Fingertips," a live recording. It captured the in-concert excitement of his singing and harp-playing, backed up by a big band. The disc turned into a million-seller, number 1 on record charts throughout the country. A hit album called *12 Year Old Genius,* Stevie's first LP, followed up this success. And as his recordings shot up the charts, Stevie skyrocketed to national fame.

Yet despite the publicity and the performing that went along with being a recording star, in many ways Stevie's life remained unchanged.

He still played with his friends as he always had. In the afternoons after school he could be seen jumping off porches and running through the neighborhood. A friend would be at his side to guide him. Or Stevie might be speeding by on a bike, his brother riding behind him to steer.

A lot of boys like to climb trees, and Stevie was no different. He liked the rough feel of the bark under his fingers and the dry sound of leaves rustling in the wind as he inched upward guided by touch alone.

Stevie played hard, but he was also a good student. He kept a solid B average. After supper he did his school work. Sometimes later at night, the sounds of the street stilled to a quiet murmur, Stevie would read to his younger brothers from his braille Bible.

Because of school, Stevie's concert appearances were usually limited to weekends. Whenever he was on the road, he always asked someone to take him shopping. He did not have a lot of money to spend — just a weekly

15

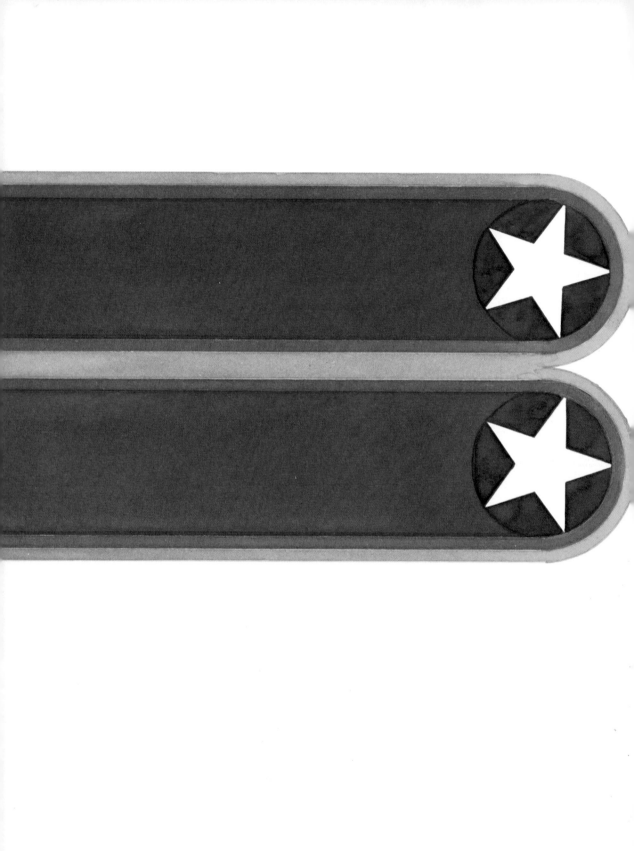

allowance of $2.50. But he always returned home with presents for his mother and his baby sister, Renee.

The people at Motown watched over Stevie's financial affairs carefully. Some of his earnings went to his family to take care of his expenses at home. All the rest of his money went into a trust fund. Within a decade Stevie would become a multi-millionaire.

As Stevie grew older, the amount of playing and travelling increased. When he reached high school age, he enrolled at the Michigan School for the Blind in Lansing. He attended classes whenever he was not touring. On the road he studied with a tutor.

At Lansing Stevie learned to read braille music and took violin, piano, and string bass lessons. His favorite of these instruments was the bass, which he played in the school orchestra. But even more than the music program, Stevie enjoyed the physical activities available at Lansing. He swam, wrestled, skated and even went bowling.

Perhaps the most important part of Stevie's education took place, not in school, but in the recording studio and on stage. He worked with some of the best pop musicians in the country and learned from their experienced advice.

His extensive touring taught him many things beside music. Stevie gained first-hand knowledge of the atmosphere and customs of other places. At age 16 he had played throughout Europe and America.

Later, Stevie would say that these early years had been very good for him. "I didn't get engulfed with people saying 'you're the greatest,' " he once remarked. "I grew up in the streets with my friends. A lot of people at Motown took good care of me. It was a very beautiful love and warmth."

Soul Music

In the mid-60's the world of pop music flowered into an incredible variety of styles. There was a constant flow of new and different music from people as diverse as the Beatles, Bob Dylan, Jimi Hendrix, the Beach Boys and the Grateful Dead.

Some of the most distinctive sounds to emerge in that era were the recordings of black artists like James Brown, Aretha Franklin, the Supremes, the Temptations and Stevie Wonder. These people refined rhythm and blues into sophisticated but highly emotional music which came to be called soul.

Soul music made a big impact on the rock scene. The drummers and bass players of bands like James Brown's introduced a new complexity into a rock rhythm. The mannerisms of soul singers began to creep into the styles of white singers. In the big cities, soul songs set the standard for danceable music.

Stevie's smash hit, "Up-tight," released in 1965, was one of the biggest trend setters. In the opening guitar line, the explosive brass, the driving beat and in Stevie's hard vocals, the song captured all the excitement of the soul era.

Stevie had written "Up-tight" himself, and increas-

18

ingly he began to record more of his own material. His sound became distinctly original.

In 1967 came another giant hit, "I Was Made To Love Her." It had a strong beat, but it still managed to be melodic — unlike some up-tempo soul songs which sounded like monotone shouting over repetitious accompaniments.

By 1967 Stevie had released a total of 9 albums and 18 singles. With so much recording experience behind him, he decided to begin producing his own records. As a producer he would have control over all aspects of the recording process. He would coordinate the efforts of the musicians, arrangers and engineers.

Stevie wanted more artistic freedom than had been allowed him in the past. Motown was in the business of turning out hits. Whenever a record sold well, they tried to repeat the formula. Their songwriters would turn out tune after tune written in styles that had worked before.

Sometimes they would record the background tracks (the guitar, bass and drum parts) for these songs — even before they knew who would be singing them. Later on, singers would add the vocals, without being able to do a thing about key, tempo or arrangements.

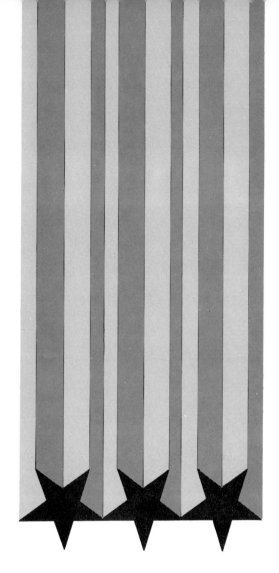

Stevie was unhappy with this assembly-line commercialism. As his own producer, he hoped to gain greater control over the sound of his records.

Towards the close of the decade, Stevie began to break away from the usual Motown sound. In 1969 he released "My Cherie Amour," a tune with a soft, mellow sound. Another hit, "For Once In My Life," was a rearrangement of a Broadway musical song.

When asked about this move away from straight soul music, Stevie replied, "I like pretty songs. Pretty tunes are coming back, tunes that are melodic, but not too melodic, tunes with melodies that stick with you."

Although he now produced most of his recordings, Stevie was still dissatisfied. He felt that his musical growth was hampered by Motown's ever-present commercial demands.

In 1971 Stevie terminated all his agreements with Motown. "I felt stagnant," he said, commenting on the decision. "I felt that what I was doing, the style that we were doing was declining. I just wanted to go somewhere else."

Stevie left Detroit and headed for New York.

Toward Inner Visions

Stevie launched into a schedule of hectic activity in New York City. Part of his days were spent in the offices of record companies where he discussed the sort of recording contract he was looking for. During many of the remaining hours, Stevie was in recording studios, taping the music he had been thinking about.

In these sessions, paid for with his own money, Stevie was totally unrestricted. He recorded the music exactly as he heard it in his head. In a burst of creative energy he completed around 40 tunes in a period of 10 days.

The recording contract he sought came unexpectedly from Motown. They offered him a new deal, one that fully met his requirements.

The first album to come out of this arrangement was *Music of My Mind*. Selected from the things that Stevie had recorded in New York, the LP was practically a solo effort. Except for guitar on one track and a trombone solo on another, Stevie played all the instruments and did all the vocals. He also composed all the music, wrote most of the lyrics and produced the album.

The result, a brand new world of sound, was like a breath of fresh air. In addition to drums, harmonica, piano, organ, bass and clavinet (an electronic keyboard instrument that sounds similar to a clavichord), Stevie played Moog and ARP synthesizers. In his hands they became an incredibly varied electronic orchestra. The total effect, in songs like "Superwoman" and "Little Girl Blue," was stunning — Stevie's fine vocals against a rich background of multi-textured electronic sounds.

However, Stevie was worried about how his new style would be accepted. Music was to him, above all else, communication between people. "Music is like a religion to me," he once said, "and the more sharing that takes place between the musicians and the audience, the more spiritual the music becomes." So Stevie wanted to make music that people could understand, since without understanding there is little basis for sharing. But he also felt that he had to explore new areas of sound and new forms of expression.

The tour with the Rolling Stones brought Stevie's new sound to a broad audience of varied tastes. Stevie found the enthusiastic reception he received encouraging. Any remaining doubts he had, melted away after he released *Talking Book,* late in 1972. This album was highlighted by the songs "You Are the Sunshine of My Life" and "Superstition," which became 2 of the biggest hits of Stevie's career.

The heavy rumble of the synthesizer bass line, the rasping metallic notes of the clavinet and the muted fire of the brass helped to create the sinister, primitive sound of "Superstition." The music fit the lyrics perfectly. The song was about the fear that comes from belief in the

supernatural: "When you believe in things that you don't understand/Then you suffer."

"Sunshine of My Life" was a classic love song — as bright in mood as "Superstition" was dark. These 2 songs revealed 2 very different sides of Stevie's personality. Moreover, they showed the wide range of styles his music included.

Stevie was maturing both as a musician and as a man. And as his talent grew, his music became more personal. His marriage of 18 months was breaking up. Songs like "Tuesday Heartbreak" and "Looking For Another Pure Love" expressed openly the pain and longing that came with the divorce.

Another aspect of Stevie's life began to come through his music. He seemed more aware of his identity as a black man. For the first time he wrote a song, "Big Brother," that dealt with race.

Stevie's sentiments about race were also revealed in what he said. He no longer liked to hear his records referred to as "soul music." For one thing, his music was moving beyond ordinary categories. But more than this, Stevie did not think that all black pop music should be lumped together as "soul."

During Stevie's childhood black music was segregated from white. Rhythm and blues was played primarily by certain radio stations that broadcast to the ghettos. Many black performers worked a circuit of clubs whose customers were all black.

The term "soul music" continued to draw a line between music for whites and music for blacks. Stevie thought this was wrong. "I like to think that the character of my sound and the music of Black people are universal," he said. "Our music should go anywhere . . . as far as the mind can go. This means making people aware of what we are about, instead of the stereotype conceptions."

In the summer of 1973 *Innervisions* was released. This album was in the style of the previous 2, but it was more polished, more sophisticated. Its overall sound was lighter and airier. The music seemed to float effortlessly.

Innervisions revealed Stevie's feelings about a wide range of things. "Living For the City" painted an angry picture of the frustrations of life in the big city ghetto.

In "Jesus Children of America" Stevie sang about the Jesus movement, revivalist churches, transcendental meditation, and drug addiction. The song subtly asked: was the spiritual salvation of currently popular religious movements real? Or was it just an illusion like the unreal high the junkie knows?

Determination to break away from the sameness of everyday life to a better spiritual state — that was the subject of "Higher Ground." Here Stevie's message was one of faith: "God is going to show you higher ground/ He's the only friend you have around."

In "Visions," Stevie's voice drifted over delicate chords that seemed to float dream-like through the air. The lyrics were as fragile as the music. They were images of a better world where people would live "hand in hand." But the song ended with a question: Can such a place ever be, "or do we have to take our wings and fly away to the visions in our mind?"

Stevie felt that this album came closest of all his records to expressing what he wanted to say as a musician. And in the album his thoughts and emotions, his inner visions were translated into remarkable music — music that told how he "saw" and responded to his world.

Innervisions revealed the maturity of Stevie's talent, the originality of his musical ideas and the beautiful and exciting manner in which he transformed those ideas into sounds.

Close of a Chapter

That summer Stevie was troubled by the strange, uneasy feeling that something was about to happen to him. He had no idea what sort of event it would be, but somehow he knew that it would signal a great change in his life.

In August, shortly after the release of *Innervisions,* his premonition violently flashed into reality. Stevie was travelling with friends on a highway outside of Winston-Salem, North Carolina. He was asleep, riding in the front seat.

The car was following closely behind a large truck, which was hauling logs. Suddenly, a chain broke loose and a huge log came hurtling at the car. Shattering glass and twisting steel, it smashed through the windshield and slammed into Stevie's forehead. In the wreckage Stevie lay motionless, unconscious and covered with blood.

He failed to regain consciousness at the hospital. His injuries were diagnosed as a fractured skull and a brain contusion (a severe bruse of the brain tissue). For days Stevie remained in a deep coma.

Finally, he showed signs that he was struggling back to consciousness. His friend Ira Tucker, Jr., was there at the bedside that day. He leaned over close to Stevie's ear and began to sing "Higher Ground": "I'm so darn glad He let me try it again 'cause my last time on earth I lived a whole world of sin." Slowly Stevie began to move his fingers in time to the music. He was on the way back.

By that winter Stevie felt strong enough to do a concert tour in England. And early in the spring at the Hollywood Paladium — the site of the Grammy Awards ceremony — it seemed that the entire American music industry was honoring Stevie's return.

The evening practically turned into "Stevie Wonder Night," as Stevie won award after award. He gave his first Grammy (for Best Rhythm and Blues Song of the Year) to his mother, who came to the stage with him to accept it.

After that Stevie won awards for Best Rhythm and Blues Vocal Performance ("Superstition"), "Best Pop Vocal Performance ("You Are the Sunshine of My Life") and Album of the Year (*Innervisions*). *Innervisions* took another Grammy as Best Engineered Recording of the Year.

At 23, Stevie already had to his credit 20 hit singles and 15 best-selling albums. The winning of 5 Grammys in one year was an unprecedented accomplishment. The awards were certainly fitting recognition of Stevie's position as one of the major talents of the contemporary music scene.

But Stevie was not about to sit back, merely enjoying his success. His brush with death the previous summer had made him intensely aware of the importance of time. "You begin to really value time, and realize the importance of doing what you have to do in as much time as you have," he said, " 'cause tomorrow is not promised to any of us."

Stevie felt that it was time to begin a new phase of his life. He believed that 1974 would be "the ending of this era in Stevie Wonder's career and the entrance to another place.''

And so the kaleidoscopic first chapter of Stevie's life was nearing its conclusion. Stevie began to make plans to go to West Africa, where drought and famine were ravaging vast areas. Stevie hoped to work with charities for deprived African children. His particular concern was for the many sightless victims of trachoma, a disease carried by certain African flies.

Stevie undertook the first step in his journey that spring, a special American concert tour to raise money for charities. Not forgetting his own people, Stevie planned to divide his donations between organizations here and in Africa. His share of the profits from the tour's opening concert at Madison Square Garden was $34,000. All of it went to a program which provides summer recreation facilities for inner-city children in New York.

In 1974 people were increasingly occupied with their own inner visions — with things like transcendental meditation, the occult, the return to simpler life-styles. It was a time when the nation as a whole seemed absorbed in its own internal problems: Watergate and the energy crisis. But Stevie was looking outward. His horizons were expanding. The images of a far-away place filled his mind.

''I have to always evolve and move ahead,'' he once remarked, ''and express to the world things that I see that people don't see; things that I feel that people don't take the time to feel; sounds that people ignore and don't hear.''

This feeling had led Stevie to create the innovative and beautiful sounds of his last 3 albums. Now it was leading him to a new and different life in a foreign land — an adventure that promised to express in yet another way the remarkable genius of Stevie Wonder.

JACKSON FIVE
CARLY SIMON
BOB DYLAN
JOHN DENVER
THE BEATLES
ELVIS PRESLEY
JOHNNY CASH
CHARLEY PRIDE
ARETHA FRANKLIN
ROBERTA FLACK
STEVIE WONDER

Rock'n PopStars